In
1935 if you
read a good book, you needed
either a lot of money or a library card.
Cheap paperbacks were available, but their
poor production generally mirrored the quality
between the covers. One weekend that year,
Allen Lane, Managing Director of The Bodley Head,
having spent the weekend visiting Agatha Christie,
found himself on a platform at Exeter station trying to
find something to read for his journey back to London.
He was appalled by the quality of the material he had to
choose from. Everything that Allen Lane achieved from that
day until his death in 1970 was based on a passionate belief
in the existence of 'a vast reading public for *intelligent*
books at a low price'. The result of his momentous vision
was the birth not only of Penguin, but of the 'paperback
revolution'. Quality writing became available for the price of
a packet of cigarettes, literature became a mass medium
for the first time, a nation of book-borrowers became a
nation of book-buyers – and the very concept of book
publishing was changed for ever. Those founding
principles – of quality and value, with an overarching
belief in the fundamental importance of reading –
have guided everything the company has
done since 1935. Sir Allen Lane's
pioneering spirit is still very much alive
at Penguin in 2005. Here's to
the next 70 years!

MORE THAN A BUSINESS

'We decided it was time to end the almost customary half-hearted manner in which cheap editions were produced – as though the only people who could possibly want cheap editions must belong to a lower order of intelligence. We, however, believed in the existence in this country of a vast reading public for intelligent books at a low price, and staked everything on it'
Sir Allen Lane, 1902–1970

'The Penguin Books are splendid value for sixpence, so splendid that if other publishers had any sense they would combine against them and suppress them'
George Orwell

'More than a business … a national cultural asset'
Guardian

'When you look at the whole Penguin achievement you know that it constitutes, in action, one of the more democratic successes of our recent social history'
Richard Hoggart

My Side of the Matter

TRUMAN CAPOTE

PENGUIN BOOKS

PENGUIN BOOKS

Published by the Penguin Group
Penguin Books Ltd, 80 Strand, London WC2R 0RL, England
Penguin Group (USA) Inc., 375 Hudson Street, New York, New York 10014, USA
Penguin Group (Canada), 10 Alcorn Avenue, Toronto, Ontario, Canada M4V 3B2
(a division of Pearson Penguin Canada Inc.)
Penguin Ireland, 25 St Stephen's Green, Dublin 2, Ireland
(a division of Penguin Books Ltd)
Penguin Group (Australia), 250 Camberwell Road, Camberwell, Victoria 3124,
Australia (a division of Pearson Australia Group Pty Ltd)
Penguin Books India Pvt Ltd, 11 Community Centre,
Panchsheel Park, New Delhi – 110 017, India
Penguin Group (NZ), cnr Airborne and Rosedale Roads, Albany,
Auckland 1310, New Zealand (a division of Pearson New Zealand Ltd)
Penguin Books (South Africa) (Pty) Ltd, 24 Sturdee Avenue,
Rosebank 2196, South Africa

Penguin Books Ltd, Registered Offices: 80 Strand, London WC2R 0RL, England

www.penguin.com

A Capote Reader first published in Great Britain by Hamish Hamilton,
by arrangement with Random House, Inc. 1987
Published in Penguin Books 1993
This selection published as a Pocket Penguin 2005

1

Set in 11.5/13.5pt Monotype Dante
Typeset by Palimpsest Book Production Limited
Polmont, Stirlingshire
Printed in England by Clays Ltd, St Ives plc

Contents

Miriam

For several years, Mrs. H. T. Miller had lived alone in a pleasant apartment (two rooms with kitchenette) in a remodeled brownstone near the East River. She was a widow: Mr. H. T. Miller had left a reasonable amount of insurance. Her interests were narrow, she had no friends to speak of, and she rarely journeyed farther than the corner grocery. The other people in the house never seemed to notice her: her clothes were matter-of-fact, her hair iron-gray, clipped and casually waved; she did not use cosmetics, her features were plain and inconspicuous, and on her last birthday she was sixty-one. Her activities were seldom spontaneous: she kept the two rooms immaculate, smoked an occasional cigarette, prepared her own meals and tended a canary.

Then she met Miriam. It was snowing that night. Mrs. Miller had finished drying the supper dishes and was thumbing through an afternoon paper when she saw an advertisement of a picture playing at a neighborhood theater. The title sounded good, so she struggled into her beaver coat, laced her galoshes and left the apartment, leaving one light burning in the foyer: she found nothing more disturbing than a sensation of darkness.

The snow was fine, falling gently, not yet making an impression on the pavement. The wind from the river cut only at street crossings. Mrs. Miller hurried, her head bowed, oblivious as a mole burrowing a blind path. She stopped at a drugstore and bought a package of peppermints.

A long line stretched in front of the box office; she took her place at the end. There would be (a tired voice groaned) a short wait for all seats. Mrs. Miller rummaged in her leather handbag till she collected exactly the correct change for admission. The line seemed to be taking its own time and, looking around for some distraction, she suddenly became conscious of a little girl standing under the edge of the marquee.

Her hair was the longest and strangest Mrs. Miller had ever seen: absolutely silver-white, like an albino's. It flowed waist-length in smooth, loose lines. She was thin and fragilely constructed. There was a simple, special elegance in the way she stood with her thumbs in the pockets of a tailored plum-velvet coat.

Mrs. Miller felt oddly excited, and when the little girl glanced toward her, she smiled warmly. The little girl walked over and said, 'Would you care to do me a favor?'

'I'd be glad to, if I can,' said Mrs. Miller.

'Oh, it's quite easy. I merely want you to buy a ticket for me; they won't let me in otherwise. Here, I have the money.' And gracefully she handed Mrs. Miller two dimes and a nickel.

They went over to the theater together. An usherette directed them to a lounge; in twenty minutes the picture would be over.

'I feel just like a genuine criminal,' said Mrs. Miller gaily, as she sat down. 'I mean, that sort of thing's against the law, isn't it? I do hope I haven't done the wrong thing. Your mother knows where you are, dear? I mean she does, doesn't she?'

The little girl said nothing. She unbuttoned her coat and folded it across her lap. Her dress underneath was prim and dark blue. A gold chain dangled about her neck, and her fingers, sensitive and musical-looking, toyed with it. Examining her more attentively, Mrs. Miller decided the truly distinctive feature was not her hair, but her eyes; they were hazel, steady, lacking any childlike quality whatsoever and, because of their size, seemed to consume her small face.

Mrs. Miller offered a peppermint. 'What's your name, dear?'

'Miriam,' she said, as though, in some curious way, it were information already familiar.

'Why, isn't that funny – my name's Miriam, too.

And it's not a terribly common name either. Now, don't tell me your last name's Miller!'

'Just Miriam.'

'But isn't that funny?'

'Moderately,' said Miriam, and rolled the peppermint on her tongue.

Mrs. Miller flushed and shifted uncomfortably. 'You have such a large vocabulary for such a little girl.'

'Do I?'

'Well, yes,' said Mrs. Miller, hastily changing the topic to: 'Do you like the movies?'

'I really wouldn't know,' said Miriam. 'I've never been before.'

Women began filling the lounge; the rumble of the newsreel bombs exploded in the distance. Mrs. Miller rose, tucking her purse under her arm. 'I guess I'd better be running now if I want to get a seat,' she said. 'It was nice to have met you.'

Miriam nodded ever so slightly.

It snowed all week. Wheels and footsteps moved soundlessly on the street, as if the business of living continued secretly behind a pale but impenetrable curtain. In the falling quiet there was no sky or earth, only snow lifting in the wind, frosting the window glass, chilling the rooms, deadening and hushing the city. At all hours it was necessary to keep a lamp lighted, and Mrs. Miller lost track of the days: Friday was no different from Saturday and on Sunday she went to the grocery: closed, of course.

That evening she scrambled eggs and fixed a bowl of tomato soup. Then, after putting on a flannel robe and cold-creaming her face, she propped herself up in bed with a hot-water bottle under her feet. She was reading the *Times* when the doorbell rang. At first she thought it must be a mistake and whoever it was would go away. But it rang and rang and settled to a persistent buzz. She looked at the clock: a little after eleven; it did not seem possible, she was always asleep by ten.

Climbing out of bed, she trotted barefoot across the living room. 'I'm coming, please be patient.' The latch was caught; she turned it this way and that way and the bell never paused an instant. 'Stop it,' she cried. The bolt gave way and she opened the door an inch. 'What in heaven's name?'

'Hello,' said Miriam.

'Oh . . . why, hello,' said Mrs. Miller, stepping hesitantly into the hall. 'You're that little girl.'

'I thought you'd never answer, but I kept my finger on the button; I knew you were home. Aren't you glad to see me?'

Mrs. Miller did not know what to say. Miriam, she saw, wore the same plum-velvet coat and now she had also a beret to match; her white hair was braided in two shining plaits and looped at the ends with enormous white ribbons.

'Since I've waited so long, you could at least let me in,' she said.

'It's awfully late. . . .'

Miriam regarded her blankly. 'What difference does that make? Let me in. It's cold out here and I have on a silk dress.' Then, with a gentle gesture, she urged Mrs. Miller aside and passed into the apartment.

She dropped her coat and beret on a chair. She was indeed wearing a silk dress. White silk. White silk in February. The skirt was beautifully pleated and the sleeves long; it made a faint rustle as she strolled about the room. 'I like your place,' she said. 'I like the rug, blue's my favorite color.' She touched a paper rose in a vase on the coffee table. 'Imitation,' she commented wanly. 'How sad. Aren't imitations sad?' She seated herself on the sofa, daintily spreading her skirt.

'What do you want?' asked Mrs. Miller.

'Sit down,' said Miriam. 'It makes me nervous to see people stand.'

Mrs. Miller sank to a hassock. 'What do you want?' she repeated.

6

'You know, I don't think you're glad I came.'

For a second time Mrs. Miller was without an answer; her hand motioned vaguely. Miriam giggled and pressed back on a mound of chintz pillows. Mrs. Miller observed that the girl was less pale than she remembered; her cheeks were flushed.

'How did you know where I lived?'

Miriam frowned. 'That's no question at all. What's your name? What's mine?'

'But I'm not listed in the phone book.'

'Oh, let's talk about something else.'

Mrs. Miller said, 'Your mother must be insane to let a child like you wander around at all hours of the night – and in such ridiculous clothes. She must be out of her mind.'

Miriam got up and moved to a corner where a covered birdcage hung from a ceiling chain. She peeked beneath the cover. 'It's a canary,' she said. 'Would you mind if I woke him? I'd like to hear him sing.'

'Leave Tommy alone,' said Mrs. Miller anxiously. 'Don't you dare wake him.'

'Certainly,' said Miriam. 'But I don't see why I can't hear him sing.' And then, 'Have you anything to eat? I'm starving! Even milk and a jam sandwich would be fine.'

'Look,' said Mrs. Miller, arising from the hassock,

'look – if I make some nice sandwiches will you be a good child and run along home? It's past midnight, I'm sure.'

'It's snowing,' reproached Miriam. 'And cold and dark.'

'Well, you shouldn't have come here to begin with,' said Mrs. Miller, struggling to control her voice. 'I can't help the weather. If you want anything to eat, you'll have to promise to leave.'

Miriam brushed a braid against her cheek. Her eyes were thoughtful, as if weighing the proposition. She turned toward the birdcage. 'Very well,' she said, 'I promise.'

How old is she? Ten? Eleven? Mrs. Miller, in the kitchen, unsealed a jar of strawberry preserves and cut four slices of bread. She poured a glass of milk and paused to light a cigarette. *And why has she come?* Her hand shook as she held the match, fascinated, till it burned her finger. The canary was singing; singing as he did in the morning and at no other time. 'Miriam,' she called, 'Miriam, I told you not to disturb Tommy.' There was no answer. She called again; all she heard was the canary. She inhaled the cigarette and discovered she had lighted the cork-tip end and – oh, really, she mustn't lose her temper.

She carried the food in on a tray and set it on

the coffee table. She saw first that the birdcage still wore its night cover. And Tommy was singing. It gave her a queer sensation. And no one was in the room. Mrs. Miller went through an alcove leading to her bedroom; at the door she caught her breath.

'What are you doing?' she asked.

Miriam glanced up and in her eyes there was a look that was not ordinary. She was standing by the bureau, a jewel case opened before her. For a minute she studied Mrs. Miller, forcing their eyes to meet, and she smiled. 'There's nothing good here,' she said. 'But I like this.' Her hand held a cameo brooch. 'It's charming.'

'Suppose – perhaps you'd better put it back,' said Mrs. Miller, feeling suddenly the need of some support. She leaned against the door frame; her head was unbearably heavy; a pressure weighted the rhythm of her heartbeat. The light seemed to flutter defectively. 'Please, child – a gift from my husband . . .'

'But it's beautiful and I want it,' said Miriam. '*Give it to me.*'

As she stood, striving to shape a sentence which would somehow save the brooch, it came to Mrs. Miller there was no one to whom she might turn; she was alone; a fact that had not been among her thoughts for a long time. Its sheer emphasis was stunning. But here in her own room in the hushed snow-city were evidences she could not ignore or, she knew with startling clarity, resist.

Miriam ate ravenously, and when the sandwiches and milk were gone, her fingers made cobweb movements over the plate, gathering crumbs. The cameo gleamed on her blouse, the blond profile like a trick reflection of its wearer. 'That was very nice,' she sighed, 'though now an almond cake or a cherry would be ideal. Sweets are lovely, don't you think?'

Mrs. Miller was perched precariously on the hassock, smoking a cigarette. Her hairnet had slipped lopsided and loose strands straggled down her face. Her eyes were stupidly concentrated on nothing and her cheeks were mottled in red patches, as though a fierce slap had left permanent marks.

'Is there a candy – a cake?'

Mrs. Miller tapped ash on the rug. Her head swayed slightly as she tried to focus her eyes. 'You promised to leave if I made the sandwiches,' she said.

'Dear me, did I?'

'It was a promise and I'm tired and I don't feel well at all.'

'Mustn't fret,' said Miriam. 'I'm only teasing.'

She picked up her coat, slung it over her arm,

and arranged her beret in front of a mirror. Presently she bent close to Mrs. Miller and whispered, 'Kiss me good night.'

'Please – I'd rather not,' said Mrs. Miller.

Miriam lifted a shoulder, arched an eyebrow. 'As you like,' she said, and went directly to the coffee table, seized the vase containing the paper roses, carried it to where the hard surface of the floor lay bare, and hurled it downward. Glass sprayed in all directions and she stamped her foot on the bouquet.

Then slowly she walked to the door, but before closing it, she looked back at Mrs. Miller with a slyly innocent curiosity.

Mrs. Miller spent the next day in bed, rising once to feed the canary and drink a cup of tea; she took her temperature and had none, yet her dreams were feverishly agitated; their unbalanced mood lingered even as she lay staring wide-eyed at the ceiling. One dream threaded through the others like an elusively mysterious theme in a complicated symphony, and the scenes it depicted were sharply outlined, as though sketched by a hand of gifted intensity: a small girl, wearing a bridal gown and a wreath of leaves, led a gray procession down a mountain path, and among them there was unusual silence till a woman at the rear asked,

'Where is she taking us?' 'No one knows,' said an old man marching in front. 'But isn't she pretty?' volunteered a third voice. 'Isn't she like a frost flower . . . so shining and white?'

Tuesday morning she woke up feeling better; harsh slats of sunlight, slanting through Venetian blinds, shed a disrupting light on her unwholesome fancies. She opened the window to discover a thawed, mild-as-spring day; a sweep of clean new clouds crumpled against a vastly blue, out-of-season sky; and across the low line of rooftops she could see the river and smoke curving from tugboat stacks in a warm wind. A great silver truck plowed the snow-banked street, its machine sound humming on the air.

After straightening the apartment, she went to the grocer's, cashed a check and continued to Schrafft's, where she ate breakfast and chatted happily with the waitress. Oh, it was a wonderful day – more like a holiday – and it would be so foolish to go home.

She boarded a Lexington Avenue bus and rode up to Eighty-sixth Street; it was here that she had decided to do a little shopping.

She had no idea what she wanted or needed, but she idled along, intent only upon the passers-by, brisk and preoccupied, who gave her a disturbing sense of separateness.

It was while waiting at the corner of Third Avenue that she saw the man: an old man, bowlegged and stooped under an armload of bulging packages; he wore a shabby brown coat and a checkered cap. Suddenly she realized they were exchanging a smile: there was nothing friendly about this smile, it was merely two cold flickers of recognition. But she was certain she had never seen him before.

He was standing next to an El pillar, and as she crossed the street he turned and followed. He kept quite close; from the corner of her eye she watched his reflection wavering on the shop-windows.

Then in the middle of the block she stopped and faced him. He stopped also and cocked his head, grinning. But what could she say? Do? Here, in broad daylight, on Eighty-sixth Street? It was useless and, despising her own helplessness, she quickened her steps.

Now Second Avenue is a dismal street, made from scraps and ends; part cobblestone, part asphalt, part cement; and its atmosphere of desertion is permanent. Mrs. Miller walked five blocks without meeting anyone, and all the while the steady crunch of his footfalls in the snow stayed near. And when she came to a florist's shop, the sound was still with her. She hurried inside and watched through the glass door as the old man passed; he kept his eyes straight ahead and didn't slow his pace, but he did one strange, telling thing: he tipped his cap.

'Six white ones, did you say?' asked the florist. 'Yes,' she told him, 'white roses.' From there she went to a glassware store and selected a vase, presumably a replacement for the one Miriam had broken, though the price was intolerable and the vase itself (she thought) grotesquely vulgar. But a series of unaccountable purchases had begun, as if by prearranged plan: a plan of which she had not the least knowledge or control.

She bought a bag of glazed cherries, and at a place called the Knickerbocker Bakery she paid forty cents for six almond cakes.

Within the last hour the weather had turned cold again; like blurred lenses, winter clouds cast a shade over the sun, and the skeleton of an early dusk colored the sky; a damp mist mixed with the wind and the voices of a few children who romped high on mountains of gutter snow seemed lonely and cheerless. Soon the first flake fell, and when Mrs. Miller reached the brownstone house, snow was falling in a swift screen and foot tracks vanished as they were printed.

★

The white roses were arranged decoratively in the vase. The glazed cherries shone on a ceramic plate. The almond cakes, dusted with sugar, awaited a hand. The canary fluttered on its swing and picked at a bar of seed.

At precisely five the doorbell rang. Mrs. Miller *knew* who it was. The hem of her housecoat trailed as she crossed the floor. 'Is that you?' she called.

'Naturally,' said Miriam, the word resounding shrilly from the hall. 'Open this door.'

'Go away,' said Mrs. Miller.

'Please hurry . . . I have a heavy package.'

'Go away,' said Mrs. Miller. She returned to the living room, lighted a cigarette, sat down and calmly listened to the buzzer; on and on and on. 'You might as well leave. I have no intention of letting you in.'

Shortly the bell stopped. For possibly ten minutes Mrs. Miller did not move. Then, hearing no sound, she concluded Miriam had gone. She tiptoed to the door and opened it a sliver; Miriam was half-reclining atop a cardboard box with a beautiful French doll cradled in her arms.

'Really, I thought you were never coming,' she said peevishly. 'Here, help me get this in, it's awfully heavy.'

It was not spell-like compulsion that Mrs. Miller felt, but rather a curious passivity; she brought in the box, Miriam, the doll. Miriam curled up on the sofa, not troubling to remove her coat or beret, and watched disinterestedly as Mrs. Miller dropped the box and stood trembling, trying to catch her breath.

'Thank you,' she said. In the daylight she looked pinched and drawn, her hair less luminous. The French doll she was loving wore an exquisite powdered wig and its idiot glass eyes sought solace in Miriam's. 'I have a surprise,' she continued. 'Look into my box.'

Kneeling, Mrs. Miller parted the flaps and lifted out another doll; then a blue dress which she recalled as the one Miriam had worn that first night at the theater; and of the remainder she said, 'It's all clothes. Why?'

'Because I've come to live with you,' said Miriam, twisting a cherry stem. 'Wasn't it nice of you to buy me the cherries . . . ?'

'But you can't! For God's sake go away – go away and leave me alone!'

'. . . and the roses and the almond cakes? How really wonderfully generous. You know, these cherries are delicious. The last place I lived was with an old man; he was terribly poor and we never had good things to eat. But I think I'll be happy here.' She paused to snuggle her doll closer. 'Now, if you'll just show me where to put my things . . .'

Mrs. Miller's face dissolved into a mask of ugly red lines; she began to cry, and it was an unnatural, tearless sort of weeping, as though, not having wept for a long time, she had forgotten how. Carefully she edged backward till she touched the door.

She fumbled through the hall and down the stairs to a landing below. She pounded frantically on the door of the first apartment she came to; a short, redheaded man answered and she pushed past him. 'Say, what the hell is this?' he said. 'Anything wrong, lover?' asked a young woman who appeared from the kitchen, drying her hands. And it was to her that Mrs. Miller turned.

'Listen,' she cried, 'I'm ashamed behaving this way but – well, I'm Mrs. H. T. Miller and I live upstairs and . . .' She pressed her hands over her face. 'It sounds so absurd. . . .'

The woman guided her to a chair, while the man excitedly rattled pocket change. 'Yeah?'

'I live upstairs and there's a little girl visiting me, and I suppose that I'm afraid of her. She won't leave and I can't make her and – she's going to do something terrible. She's already stolen my cameo, but she's about to do something worse – something terrible!'

The man asked, 'Is she a relative, huh?'

Mrs. Miller shook her head. 'I don't know who she is. Her name's Miriam, but I don't know for certain who she is.'

'You gotta calm down, honey,' said the woman, stroking Mrs. Miller's arm. 'Harry here'll tend to this kid. Go on, lover.' And Mrs. Miller said, 'The door's open – 5A.'

After the man left, the woman brought a towel and bathed Mrs. Miller's face. 'You're very kind,' Mrs. Miller said. 'I'm sorry to act like such a fool, only this wicked child . . .'

'Sure, honey,' consoled the woman. 'Now, you better take it easy.'

Mrs. Miller rested her head in the crook of her arm; she was quiet enough to be asleep. The woman turned a radio dial; a piano and a husky voice filled the silence and the woman, tapping her foot, kept excellent time. 'Maybe we oughta go up too,' she said.

'I don't want to see her again. I don't want to be anywhere near her.'

'Uh huh, but what you shoulda done, you shoulda called a cop.'

Presently they heard the man on the stairs. He strode into the room frowning and scratching the back of his neck. 'Nobody there,' he said, honestly embarrassed. 'She musta beat it.'

'Harry, you're a jerk,' announced the woman.

'We been sitting here the whole time and we woulda seen . . .' she stopped abruptly, for the man's glance was sharp.

'I looked all over,' he said, 'and there just ain't nobody there. Nobody, understand?'

'Tell me,' said Mrs. Miller, rising, 'tell me, did you see a large box? Or a doll?'

'No, ma'am, I didn't.'

And the woman, as if delivering a verdict, said, 'Well, for cryinoutloud. . . .'

Mrs. Miller entered her apartment softly; she walked to the center of the room and stood quite still. No, in a sense it had not changed: the roses, the cakes, and the cherries were in place. But this was an empty room, emptier than if the furnishings and familiars were not present, lifeless and petrified as a funeral parlor. The sofa loomed before her with a new strangeness: its vacancy had a meaning that would have been less penetrating and terrible had Miriam been curled on it. She gazed fixedly at the space where she remembered setting the box and, for a moment, the hassock spun desperately. And she looked through the window; surely the river was real, surely snow was falling – but then, one could not be certain witness to anything: Miriam, so vividly there – and yet, where was she? Where, where?

As though moving in a dream, she sank to a chair. The room was losing shape; it was dark and getting darker and there was nothing to be done about it; she could not lift her hand to light a lamp.

Suddenly, closing her eyes, she felt an upward surge, like a diver emerging from some deeper, greener depth. In times of terror or immense distress, there are moments when the mind waits, as though for a revelation, while a skein of calm is woven over thought; it is like a sleep, or a supernatural trance; and during this lull one is aware of a force of quiet reasoning: well, what if she had never really known a girl named Miriam? that she had been foolishly frightened on the street? In the end, like everything else, it was of no importance. For the only thing she had lost to Miriam was her identity, but now she knew she had found again the person who lived in this room, who cooked her own meals, who owned a canary, who was someone she could trust and believe in: Mrs. H. T. Miller.

Listening in contentment, she became aware of a double sound: a bureau drawer opening and closing; she seemed to hear it long after completion – opening and closing. Then gradually, the harshness of it was replaced by the murmur of a silk dress and this, delicately faint, was moving nearer and swelling in intensity till the walls trembled with the vibration and the room was caving under a wave of whispers. Mrs. Miller stiffened and opened her eyes to a dull, direct stare.

'Hello,' said Miriam.

My Side of the Matter

I know what is being said about me and you can take my side or theirs, that's your own business. It's my word against Eunice's and Olivia-Ann's, and it should be plain enough to anyone with two good eyes which one of us has their wits about them. I just want the citizens of the U.S.A. to know the facts, that's all.

The facts: On Sunday, August 12, this year of our Lord, Eunice tried to kill me with her papa's Civil War sword and Olivia-Ann cut up all over the place with a fourteen-inch hog knife. This is not even to mention lots of other things.

It began six months ago when I married Marge. That was the first thing I did wrong. We were married in Mobile after an acquaintance of only four days. We were both sixteen and she was visiting my cousin Georgia. Now that I've had plenty of time to think it over, I can't for the life of me figure how I fell for the likes of her. She has no looks, no body and no brains whatsoever. But Marge is a natural blonde and maybe that's the answer. Well, we were married going on three

23

months when Marge ups and gets pregnant; the second thing I did wrong. Then she starts hollering that she's got to go home to Mama – only she hasn't got no mama, just these two aunts. Eunice and Olivia-Ann. So she makes me quit my perfectly swell position clerking at the Cash 'n' Carry and move here to Admiral's Mill, which is nothing but a damn gap in the road any way you care to consider it.

The day Marge and I got off the train at the L&N depot it was raining cats and dogs and do you think anyone came to meet us? I'd shelled out forty-one cents for a telegram, too! Here my wife's pregnant and we have to tramp seven miles in a downpour. It was bad on Marge, as I couldn't carry hardly any of our stuff on account of I have terrible trouble with my back. When I first caught sight of this house I must say I was impressed. It's big and yellow and has real columns out in front and japonica trees, both red and white, lining the yard.

Eunice and Olivia-Ann had seen us coming and were waiting in the hall. I swear I wish you could get a look at these two. Honest, you'd die! Eunice is this big old fat thing with a behind that must weigh a tenth of a ton. She troops around the house, rain or shine, in this real old-fashioned nightie, calls it a kimono, but it isn't anything in this world but a dirty flannel nightie. Furthermore she chews tobacco and tries to pretend so ladylike, spitting on the sly. She keeps gabbing about what a fine education she had, which is her way of attempting to make me feel bad, although, personally, it never bothers me so much as one whit, as I know for a fact she can't even read the funnies without she spells out every single, solitary word. You've got to hand her one thing, though – she can add and subtract money so fast that there's no doubt but what she could be up in Washington, D.C., working where they make the stuff. Not that she hasn't got plenty of money! Naturally she says she hasn't but I know she has because one day, accidentally, I happened to find close to a thousand dollars hidden in a flowerpot on the side porch. I didn't touch one cent, only Eunice says I stole a hundred-dollar bill, which is a venomous lie from start to finish. Of course anything Eunice says is an order from headquarters, as not a breathing soul in Admiral's Mill can stand up and say he doesn't owe her money and if she said Charlie Carson (a blind ninety-year-old invalid who hasn't taken a step since 1896) threw her on her back and raped her, everybody in this county would swear the same on a stack of Bibles.

Now, Olivia-Ann is worse, and that's the truth! Only she's not so bad on the nerves as Eunice, for she is a natural-born half-wit and ought really to be kept in somebody's attic. She's real pale and skinny and has a mustache. She squats around most of the time whittling on a stick with her fourteen-inch hog knife, otherwise she's up to some devilment, like what she did to Mrs. Harry Steller Smith. I swore not ever to tell anyone that, but when a vicious attempt has been made on a person's life, I say the hell with promises.

Mrs. Harry Steller Smith was Eunice's canary named after a woman from Pensacola who makes home-made cure-all that Eunice takes for the gout. One day I heard this terrible racket in the parlor and upon investigating, what did I find but Olivia-Ann shooing Mrs. Harry Steller Smith out an open window with a broom and the door to the bird-cage wide. If I hadn't walked in at exactly that moment, she might never have been caught. She got scared that I would tell Eunice and blurted out the whole thing, said it wasn't fair to keep one of God's creatures locked up that way, besides which she couldn't stand Mrs. Harry Steller Smith's singing. Well, I felt kind of sorry for her and she gave me two dollars, so I helped her cook up a story for Eunice. Of course I wouldn't have taken the money except I thought it would ease her conscience.

The very *first* words Eunice said when I stepped

inside this house were, 'So this is what you ran off behind our back and married, Marge?'

Marge says, 'Isn't he the best-looking thing, Aunt Eunice?'

Eunice eyes me u-p and d-o-w-n and says, 'Tell him to turn around.'

While my back is turned, Eunice says, 'You sure must've picked the runt of the litter. Why, this isn't any sort of man at all.'

I've never been so taken back in my life! True, I'm slightly stocky, but then, I haven't got my full growth yet.

'He is too,' says Marge.

Olivia-Ann, who's been standing there with her mouth so wide the flies could buzz in and out, says, 'You heard what Sister said. He's not any sort of a man whatsoever. The very idea of this little runt running around claiming to be a man! Why, he isn't even of the male sex!'

Marge says, 'You seem to forget, Aunt Olivia-Ann, that this is my husband, the father of my unborn child.'

Eunice made a nasty sound like only she can and said, 'Well, all I can say is I most certainly wouldn't be bragging about it.'

Isn't that a nice welcome? And after I gave up my perfectly swell position clerking at the Cash 'n' Carry.

But it's not a drop in the bucket to what came later that same evening. After Bluebell cleared away the supper dishes, Marge asked, just as nice as she could, if we could borrow the car and drive over to the picture show at Phoenix City.

'You must be clear out of your head,' says Eunice, and, honest, you'd think we'd asked for the kimono off her back.

'You must be clear out of your head,' says Olivia-Ann.

'It's six o'clock,' says Eunice, 'and if you think I'd let that runt drive my just-as-good-as-brand-new 1934 Chevrolet as far as the privy and back, you must've gone clear out of your head.'

Naturally such language makes Marge cry.

'Never you mind, honey,' I said, 'I've driven pulenty of Cadillacs in my time.'

'Humf,' says Eunice.

'Yeah,' says I.

Eunice says, 'If he's ever so much as driven a plow, I'll eat a dozen gophers fried in turpentine.'

'I won't have you refer to my husband in any such manner,' says Marge. 'You're acting simply outlandish! Why, you'd think I'd picked up some absolutely strange man in some absolutely strange place.'

'If the shoe fits, wear it!' says Eunice.

'Don't think you can pull the sheep over our

28

eyes,' says Olivia-Ann in that braying voice of hers so much like the mating call of a jackass you can't rightly tell the difference.

'We weren't born just around the corner, you know,' says Eunice.

Marge says, 'I'll give you to understand that I'm legally wed till death do us part to this man by a certified justice of the peace as of three and one-half months ago. Ask anybody. Furthermore, Aunt Eunice, he is free, white and sixteen. Furthermore, George Far Sylvester does not appreciate hearing his father referred to in any such manner.'

George Far Sylvester is the name we've planned for the baby. Has a strong sound, don't you think? Only the way things stand I have positively no feelings in the matter now whatsoever.

'How can a girl have a baby with a girl?' says Olivia-Ann, which was a calculated attack on my manhood. 'I do declare there's something new every day.'

'Oh, shush up,' says Eunice. 'Let us hear no more about the picture show in Phoenix City.'

Marge sobs, 'Oh-h-h, but it's Judy Garland.'

'Never mind, honey,' I said, 'I most likely saw the show in Mobile ten years ago.'

'That's a deliberate falsehood,' shouts Olivia-Ann. 'Oh, you are a scoundrel, you are. Judy hasn't been in the pictures ten years.' Olivia-Ann's never seen not even one picture show in her entire fifty-two years (she won't tell anybody how old she is but I dropped a card to the capitol in Montgomery and they were very nice about answering), but she subscribes to eight movie books. According to Postmistress Delancey, it's the only mail she ever gets outside of the Sears & Roebuck. She has this positively morbid crush on Gary Cooper and has one trunk and two suitcases full of his photos.

So we got up from the table and Eunice lumbers over to the window and looks out to the chinaberry tree and says, 'Birds settling in their roost – time we went to bed. You have your old room, Marge, and I've fixed a cot for this gentleman on the back porch.'

It took a solid minute for that to sink in.

I said, 'And what, if I'm not too bold to ask, is the objection to my sleeping with my lawful wife?'

Then they both started yelling at me.

So Marge threw a conniption fit right then and there. 'Stop it, stop it, stop it! I can't stand any more. Go on, babydoll – go on and sleep whatever they say. Tomorrow we'll see. . . .'

Eunice says, 'I swanee if the child hasn't got a grain of sense, after all.'

'Poor dear,' says Olivia-Ann, wrapping her arm

around Marge's waist and herding her off, 'poor dear, so young, so innocent. Let's us just go and have a good cry on Olivia-Ann's shoulder.'

May, June and July and the best part of August I've squatted and sweltered on that damn back porch without an ounce of screening. And Marge – she hasn't opened her mouth in protest, not once! This part of Alabama is swampy, with mosquitoes that could murder a buffalo, given half a chance, not to mention dangerous flying roaches and a posse of local rats big enough to haul a wagon train from here to Timbuctoo. Oh, if it wasn't for that little unborn George, I would've been making dust tracks on the road, way before now. I mean to say I haven't had five seconds alone with Marge since that first night. One or the other is always chaperoning and last week they like to have blown their tops when Marge locked herself in her room and they couldn't find me nowhere. The truth is I'd been down watching the niggers bale cotton but just for spite I let on to Eunice like Marge and I'd been up to no good. After that they added Bluebell to the shift.

And all this time I haven't even had cigarette change.

Eunice has hounded me day in and day out about getting a job. 'Why don't the little heathen go out and get some honest work?' says she. As you've probably noticed, she never speaks to me directly, though more often than not I am the only one in her royal presence. 'If he was any sort of man you could call a man, he'd be trying to put a crust of bread in that girl's mouth instead of stuffing his own off my vittles.' I think you should know that I've been living almost exclusively on cold yams and leftover grits for three months and thirteen days and I've been down to consult Dr. A. N. Carter twice. He's not exactly sure whether I have the scurvy or not.

And as for my not working, I'd like to know what a man of my abilities, a man who held a perfectly swell position with the Cash 'n' Carry, would find to do in a fleabag like Admiral's Mill? There is all of one store here and Mr. Tubberville, the proprietor, is actually so lazy it's painful for him to have to sell anything. Then we have the Morning Star Baptist Church but they already have a preacher, an awful old turd named Shell whom Eunice drug over one day to see about the salvation of my soul. I heard him with my own ears tell her I was too far gone.

But it's what Eunice has done to Marge that really takes the cake. She has turned that girl against me in the most villainous fashion that words could not describe. Why, she even reached the point when she was sassing me back, but I provided her with a couple of good slaps and put a stop to that. No wife of mine is ever going to be disrespectful to me, not on your life!

The enemy lines are stretched tight: Bluebell, Olivia-Ann, Eunice, Marge and the whole rest of Admiral's Mill (pop. 342). Allies: none. Such was the situation as of Sunday, August 12, when the attempt was made upon my very life.

Yesterday was quiet and hot enough to melt rock. The trouble began at exactly two o'clock. I know because Eunice has one of those fool cuckoo contraptions and it scares the daylights out of me. I was minding my own personal business in the parlor, composing a song on the upright piano, which Eunice bought for Olivia-Ann and hired her a teacher to come all the way from Columbus, Georgia, once a week. Postmistress Delancey, who was my friend till she decided that it was maybe not so wise, says that the fancy teacher tore out of this house one afternoon like old Adolf Hitler was on his tail and leaped in his Ford coupé, never to be heard from again. Like I say, I'm trying to keep cool in the parlor not bothering a living soul when Olivia-Ann trots in with her hair all twisted up in curlers and shrieks, 'Cease that infernal racket this very instant! Can't you give a body a minute's rest? And get off my piano right smart. It's not your piano, it's my piano, and if you don't get off it right smart, I'll have you in court like a shot the first Monday in September.'

She's not anything in this world but jealous on account of I'm a natural-born musician and the songs I make up out of my own head are absolutely marvelous.

'And just look what you've done to my genuine ivory keys, Mr. Sylvester,' says she, trotting over to the piano, 'torn nearly every one of them off right at the roots for purentee meanness, that's what you've done.'

She knows good and well that the piano was ready for the junk heap the moment I entered this house.

I said, 'Seeing as you're such a know-it-all, Miss Olivia-Ann, maybe it would interest you to know that I'm in the possession of a few interesting tales myself. A few things that maybe other people would be very grateful to know. Like what happened to Mrs. Harry Steller Smith, as for instance.'

Remember Mrs. Harry Steller Smith?

She paused and looked at the empty birdcage. 'You gave me your oath,' says she and turned the most terrifying shade of purple.

'Maybe I did and again maybe I didn't,' says I. 'You did an evil thing when you betrayed Eunice that way but if some people will leave other people alone, then maybe I can overlook it.'

Well, sir, she walked out of there just as *nice* and *quiet* as you please. So I went and stretched out on the sofa, which is the most horrible piece of furniture I've ever seen and is part of a matched set Eunice bought in Atlanta in 1912 and paid two thousand dollars for, cash – or so she claims. This set is black and olive plush and smells like wet chicken feathers on a damp day. There is a big table in one corner of the parlor which supports two pictures of Miss E and O-A's mama and papa. Papa is kind of handsome but just between you and me I'm convinced he has black blood in him from somewhere. He was a captain in the Civil War and that is one thing I'll never forget on account of his sword, which is displayed over the mantel and figures prominently in the action yet to come. Mama has that hang-dog, half-wit look like Olivia-Ann, though I must say Mama carries it better.

So I had just dozed off when I heard Eunice bellowing, 'Where is he? Where is he?' And the next thing I know she's framed in the doorway with her hands planted plumb on those hippo hips and the whole pack scrunched up behind her: Bluebell, Olivia-Ann and Marge.

Several seconds passed with Eunice tapping her big old bare foot just as fast and furious as she could and fanning her fat face with this cardboard picture of Niagara Falls.

'Where is it?' says she. 'Where's my hundred dollars that he made away with while my trusting back was turned?'

'*This* is the straw that broke the camel's back,' says I, but I was too hot and tired to get up.

'That's not the only back that's going to be broke,' says she, her bug eyes about to pop clear out of their sockets. 'That was my funeral money and I want it back. Wouldn't you know he'd steal from the dead?'

'Maybe he didn't take it,' says Marge.

'You keep your mouth out of this, missy,' says Olivia-Ann.

'He stole my money sure as shooting,' says Eunice. 'Why, look at his eyes – black with guilt!'

I yawned and said, 'Like they say in the courts – if the party of the first part falsely accuses the party of the second part, then the party of the first part can be locked away in jail even if the State Home is where they rightfully belong for the protection of all concerned.'

'God will punish him,' says Eunice.

'Oh, Sister,' says Olivia-Ann, 'let us not wait for God.'

Whereupon Eunice advances on me with this most peculiar look, her dirty flannel nightie jerking along the floor. And Olivia-Ann leeches after her and Bluebell lets forth this moan that must have been heard clear to Eufala and back while Marge stands there wringing her hands and whimpering.

'Oh-h-h,' sobs Marge, 'please give her back that money, babydoll.'

I said, 'Et tu Brute?' which is from William Shakespeare.

'Look at the likes of him,' says Eunice, 'lying around all day not doing so much as licking a postage stamp.'

'Pitiful,' clucks Olivia-Ann.

'You'd think he was having a baby instead of that poor child.' Eunice speaking.

Bluebell tosses in her two cents, 'Ain't it the truth?'

'Well, if it isn't the old pots calling the kettle black,' says I.

'After loafing here for three months, does this runt have the audacity to cast aspersions in my direction?' says Eunice.

I merely flicked a bit of ash from my sleeve and not the least bit fazed said, 'Dr. A. N. Carter has informed me that I am in a dangerous scurvy condition and can't stand the least excitement whatsoever – otherwise I'm liable to foam at the mouth and bite somebody.'

Then Bluebell says, 'Why don't he go back to that trash in Mobile, Miss Eunice? I'se sick and tired of carryin' his ol' slop jar.'

Naturally that coal-black nigger made me so mad I couldn't see straight.

So just as calm as a cucumber I arose and picked up this umbrella off the hat tree and rapped her across the head with it until it cracked smack in two.

'My real Japanese silk parasol!' shrieks Olivia-Ann.

Marge cries, 'You've killed Bluebell, you've killed poor old Bluebell!'

Eunice shoves Olivia-Ann and says, 'He's gone clear out of his head, Sister! Run! Run and get Mr. Tubberville!'

'I don't like Mr. Tubberville,' says Olivia-Ann staunchly. 'I'll go get my hog knife.' And she makes a dash for the door, but seeing as I care nothing for death, I brought her down with a sort of tackle. It wrenched my back something terrible.

'He's going to kill her!' hollers Eunice loud enough to bring the house down. 'He's going to murder us all! I warned you, Marge. Quick, child, get Papa's sword!'

So Marge gets Papa's sword and hands it to Eunice. Talk about wifely devotion! And, if that's not bad enough, Olivia-Ann gives me this terrific knee punch and I had to let go. The next thing you know we hear her out in the yard bellowing hymns.

*Mine eyes have seen the glory of the
          coming of the Lord;
He is trampling out the vintage where
          the grapes of wrath are stored. . . .*

Meanwhile, Eunice is sashaying all over the place, wildly thrashing Papa's sword, and somehow I've managed to clamber atop the piano. Then Eunice climbs up on the piano stool and how that rickety contraption survived a monster like her I'll never be the one to tell.

'Come down from there, you yellow coward, before I run you through,' says she and takes a whack and I've got a half-inch cut to prove it.

By this time Bluebell has recovered and skittered away to join Olivia-Ann holding services in the front yard. I guess they were expecting my body and God knows it would've been theirs if Marge hadn't passed out cold.

That's the only good thing I've got to say for Marge.

What happened after that I can't rightly remember except for Olivia-Ann reappearing with her fourteen-inch hog knife and a bunch of the neighbors. But suddenly Marge was the star attraction and I suppose they carried her to her room. Anyway, as soon as they left I barricaded the parlor door.

I've got all those black and olive plush chairs pushed against it and that big mahogany table that must weigh a couple of tons and the hat tree and lots of other stuff. I've locked the windows and pulled down the shades. Also I've found a five-pound box of Sweet Love candy and this very minute I'm munching a juicy, creamy, chocolate cherry. Sometimes they come to the door and knock and yell and plead. Oh, yes, they've started singing a song of a very different color. But as for me – I give them a tune on the piano every now and then just to let them know I'm cheerful.

Music for Chameleons

She is tall and slender, perhaps seventy, silver-haired, soigné, neither black nor white, a pale golden rum color. She is a Martinique aristocrat who lives in Fort de France but also has an apartment in Paris. We are sitting on the terrace of her house, an airy, elegant house that looks as if it were made of wooden lace: it reminds me of certain old New Orleans houses. We are drinking iced mint tea slightly flavored with absinthe.

Three green chameleons race one another across the terrace; one pauses at Madame's feet, flicking its forked tongue, and she comments: 'Chameleons. Such exceptional creatures. The way they change color. Red. Yellow. Lime. Pink. Lavender. And did you know they are very fond of music?' She regards me with her fine black eyes. 'You don't believe me?'

During the course of the afternoon she had told me many curious things. How at night her garden was filled with mammoth night-flying moths. That her chauffeur, a dignified figure who had driven me to her house in a dark green Mercedes, was a wife-poisoner who had escaped from Devil's Island. And she had described a village high in the northern mountains that is entirely inhabited by albinos: 'Little pink-eyed people white as chalk. Occasionally one sees a few on the streets of Fort de France.'

'Yes, of course I believe you.'

She tilts her silver head. 'No, you don't. But I shall prove it.'

So saying, she drifts into her cool Caribbean salon, a shadowy room with gradually turning ceiling fans, and poses herself at a well-tuned piano. I am still sitting on the terrace, but I can observe her, this chic, elderly woman, the product of varied bloods. She begins to perform a Mozart sonata.

Eventually the chameleons accumulated: a dozen, a dozen more, most of them green, some scarlet, lavender. They skittered across the terrace and scampered into the salon, a sensitive, absorbed audience for the music played. And then not played, for suddenly my hostess stood and stamped her foot, and the chameleons scattered like sparks from an exploding star.

Now she regards me. '*Et maintenant? C'est vrai?*'

'Indeed. But it seems so strange.'

She smiles. '*Alors*. The whole island floats in strangeness. This very house is haunted. Many ghosts dwell here. And not in darkness. Some appear in the bright light of noon, saucy as you please. Impertinent.'

'That's common in Haiti, too. The ghosts there often stroll about in daylight. I once saw a horde of ghosts working in a field near Petionville. They were picking bugs off coffee plants.'

She accepts this as fact, and continues: '*Oui. Oui.* The Haitians work their dead. They are well known for that. Ours we leave to their sorrows. And their frolics. So coarse, the Haitians. So Creole. And one can't bathe there, the sharks are so intimidating. And their mosquitoes: the size, the audacity! Here in Martinique we have no mosquitoes. None.'

'I've noticed that; I wondered about it.'

'So do we. Martinique is the only island in the Caribbean not cursed with mosquitoes, and no one can explain it.'

'Perhaps the night-flying moths devour them all.'

She laughs. 'Or the ghosts.'

'No. I think ghosts would prefer moths.'

'Yes, moths are perhaps more ghostly fodder. If I was a hungry ghost, I'd rather eat anything than mosquitoes. Will you have more ice in your glass? Absinthe?'

'Absinthe. That's something we can't get at home. Not even in New Orleans.'

'My paternal grandmother was from New Orleans.'

'Mine, too.'

As she pours absinthe from a dazzling emerald decanter: 'Then perhaps we are related. Her maiden name was Dufont. Alouette Dufont.'

'Alouette? Really? Very pretty. I'm aware of two Dufont families in New Orleans, but I'm not related to either of them.'

'Pity. It would have been amusing to call you cousin. *Alors*. Claudine Paulot tells me this is your first visit to Martinique.'

'Claudine Paulot?'

'Claudine and Jacques Paulot. You met them at the Governor's dinner the other night.'

I remember: he was a tall, handsome man, the First President of the Court of Appeals for Martinique and French Guiana, which includes Devil's Island. 'The Paulots. Yes. They have eight children. He very much favors capital punishment.'

'Since you seem to be a traveler, why have you not visited here sooner?'

'Martinique? Well, I felt a certain reluctance. A good friend was murdered here.'

Madame's lovely eyes are a fraction less friendly than before. She makes a slow pronouncement: 'Murder is a rare occurrence here. We are not a violent people. Serious, but not violent.'

44

'Serious. Yes. The people in restaurants, on the streets, even on the beaches have such severe expressions. They seem so preoccupied. Like Russians.'

'One must keep in mind that slavery did not end here until 1848.'

I fail to make the connection, but do not inquire, for already she is saying: 'Moreover, Martinique is *très cher*. A bar of soap bought in Paris for five francs costs twice that here. The price of everything is double what it should be because everything has to be imported. If these trouble-makers got their way, and Martinique became independent of France, then that would be the close of it. Martinique could not exist without subsidy from France. We would simply perish. *Alors*, some of us have serious expressions. Generally speaking, though, do you find the population attractive?'

'The women. I've seen some amazingly beautiful women. Supple, suave, such beautifully haughty postures; bone structure as fine as cats. Also, they have a certain alluring aggressiveness.'

'That's the Senegalese blood. We have much Senegalese here. But the men – you do not find them so appealing?'

'No.'

'I agree. The men are not appealing. Compared

to our women, they seem irrelevant, without character: *vin ordinaire*. Martinique, you understand, is
a matriarchal society. When that is the case, as it
is in India, for example, then the men never
amount to much. I see you are looking at my black
mirror.'

I am. My eyes distractedly consult it – are drawn
to it against my will, as they sometimes are by the
senseless flickerings of an unregulated television
set. It has that kind of frivolous power. Therefore,
I shall overly describe it – in the manner of those
'avant-garde' French novelists who, having chosen
to discard narrative, character and structure,
restrict themselves to page-length paragraphs
detailing the contours of a single object, the
mechanics of an isolated movement: a wall, a white
wall with fly meandering across it. So: the object
in Madame's drawing room is a black mirror. It is
seven inches tall and six inches wide. It is framed
within a worn black leather case that is shaped like
a book. Indeed, the case is lying open on a table,
just as though it were a deluxe edition meant to
be picked up and browsed through; but there is
nothing there to be read or seen – except the
mystery of one's own image projected by the black
mirror's surface before it recedes into its endless
depths, its corridors of darkness.

'It belonged,' she is explaining, 'to Gauguin. You

know, of course, that he lived and painted here before he settled among the Polynesians. That was his black mirror. They were a quite common artifact among artists of the last century. Van Gogh used one. As did Renoir.'

'I don't quite understand. What did they use them for?'

'To refresh their vision. Renew their reaction to color, the tonal variations. After a spell of work, their eyes fatigued, they rested themselves by gazing into these dark mirrors. Just as gourmets at a banquet, between elaborate courses, reawaken their palates with a *sorbet de citron*.' She lifts the small volume containing the mirror off the table and passes it to me. 'I often use it when my eyes have been stricken by too much sun. It's soothing.'

Soothing, and also disquieting. The blackness, the longer one gazes into it, ceases to be black, but becomes a queer silver-blue, the threshold to secret visions; like Alice, I feel on the edge of a voyage through a looking-glass, one I'm hesitant to take.

From a distance I hear her voice – smoky, serene, cultivated: 'And so you had a friend who was murdered here?'

'Yes.'

'An American?'

'Yes. He was a very gifted man. A musician. A composer.'

'Oh, I remember – the man who wrote operas! Jewish. He had a mustache.'

'His name was Marc Blitzstein.'

'But that was long ago. At least fifteen years. Or more. I understand you are staying at the new hotel. La Bataille. How do you find it?'

'Very pleasant. In a bit of a turmoil because they are in the process of opening a casino. The man in charge of the casino is called Shelley Keats. I thought it was a joke at first, but that really happens to be his name.'

'Marcel Proust works at Le Foulard, that fine little seafood restaurant in Schoelcher, the fishing village. Marcel is a waiter. Have you been disappointed in our restaurants?'

'Yes and no. They're better than anywhere else in the Caribbean, but too expensive.'

'*Alors.* As I remarked, everything is imported. We don't even grow our own vegetables. The natives are too lackadaisical.' A hummingbird penetrates the terrace and casually balances on the air. 'But our sea-fare is exceptional.'

'Yes and no. I've never seen such enormous lobsters. Absolute whales; prehistoric creatures. I ordered one, but it was tasteless as chalk, and so tough to chew that I lost a filling. Like California fruit: splendid to look at, but without flavor.'

She smiles, not happily: 'Well, I apologize' – and

I regret my criticism, and realize I'm not being very gracious.

'I had lunch at your hotel last week. On the terrace overlooking the pool. I was shocked.'

'How so?'

'By the bathers. The foreign ladies gathered around the pool wearing nothing above and very little below. Do they permit that in your country? Virtually naked women parading themselves?'

'Not in so public a place as a hotel pool.'

'Exactly. And I don't think it should be condoned here. But of course we can't afford to annoy the tourists. Have you bothered with any of our tourist attractions?'

'We went yesterday to see the house where Empress Josephine was born.'

'I never advise anyone to visit there. That old man, the curator, what a chatterbox! And I can't say which is worse – his French or his English or his German. Such a bore. As though the journey getting there weren't tiring enough.'

Our hummingbird departs. Far off we hear steel-drum bands, tambourines, drunken choirs (*'Ce soir, ce soir nous danserons sans chemise, sans pantalons'*: Tonight, tonight we dance without shirts, without pants), sounds reminding us that it is Carnival week in Martinique.

'Usually,' she announces, 'I leave the island

during Carnival. It's impossible. The racket, the
stench.'

When planning for this Martinique experience,
which included traveling with three companions, I
had not known our visit would coincide with
Carnival; as a New Orleans native, I've had my fill
of such affairs. However, the Martinique variation
proved surprisingly vital, spontaneous and vivid as
a bomb explosion in a fireworks factory. 'We're
enjoying it, my friends and I. Last night there was
one marvelous marching group: fifty men carrying
black umbrellas and wearing silk tophats and with
their torsos painted with phosphorescent skeleton
bones. I love the old ladies with gold-tinsel wigs
and sequins pasted all over their faces. And all those
men wearing their wives' white wedding gowns!
And the millions of children holding candles,
glowing like fireflies. Actually, we did have one
near-disaster. We borrowed a car from the hotel,
and just as we arrives in Fort de France, and were
creeping through the midst of the crowds, one of
our tires blew out, and immediately we were
surrounded by red devils with pitchforks –'

Madame is amused: '*Oui. Oui.* The little boys
who dress as red devils. That goes back centuries.'

'Yes, but they were dancing all over the car. Doing
terrific damage. The roof was a positive samba floor.
But we couldn't abandon it, for fear they'd wreck it

altogether. So the calmest of my friends, Bob MacBride, volunteered to change the tire then and there. The problem was that he had on a new white linen suit and didn't want to ruin it.'

'Therefore, he disrobed. Very sensible.'

'At least it was funny. To watch MacBride, who's quite a solemn sort of fellow, stripped to his briefs and trying to change a tire with Mardi Gras madness swirling around him and red devils jabbing at him with pitchforks. Paper pitchforks, luckily.'

'But Mr. MacBride succeeded.'

'If he hadn't, I doubt that I'd be here abusing your hospitality.'

'Nothing would have happened. We are not a violent people.'

'Please. I'm not suggesting we were in any danger. It was just – well, part of the fun.'

'Absinthe? *Un peu?*'

'A mite. Thank you.'

The hummingbird returns.

'Your friend, the composer?'

'Marc Blitzstein.'

'I've been thinking. He came here once to dinner. Madame Derain brought him. And Lord Snowdon was here that evening. With his uncle, the Englishman who built all those houses on Mustique –'

'Oliver Messel.'

'*Oui. Oui.* It was while my husband was still alive. My husband had a fine ear for music. He asked your friend to play the piano. He played some German songs.' She is standing now, moving to and fro, and I am aware of how exquisite her figure is, how ethereal it seems silhouetted inside a frail green lace Parisian dress. 'I remember that, yet I can't recall how he died. Who killed him?'

All the while the black mirror has been lying in my lap, and once more my eyes seek its depths. Strange where our passions carry us, floggingly pursue us, forcing upon us unwanted dreams, unwelcome destinies.

'Two sailors.'

'From here? Martinique?'

'No. Two Portuguese sailors off a ship that was in harbor. He met them in a bar. He was here working on an opera, and he'd rented a house. He took them home with him –'

'I *do* remember. They robbed him and beat him to death. It was dreadful. An appalling tragedy.'

'A tragic accident.' The black mirror mocks me: Why did you say that? It wasn't an accident.

'But our police caught those sailors. They were tried and sentenced and sent to prison in Guiana. I wonder if they are still there. I might ask Paulot. He would know. After all, he is the First President of the Court of Appeals.'

'It really doesn't matter.'

'Not matter! Those wretches ought to have been guillotined.'

'No. But I wouldn't mind seeing them at work in the fields in Haiti, picking bugs off coffee plants.'

Raising my eyes from the mirror's demonic shine, I notice my hostess has momentarily retreated from the terrace into her shadowy salon. A piano chord echoes, and another. Madame is toying with the same tune. Soon the music lovers assemble, chameleons scarlet, green, lavender, an audience that, lined out on the floor of the terra-cotta terrace, resembles a written arrangement of musical notes. A Mozartean mosaic.

Mr. Jones

During the winter of 1945 I lived in Brooklyn. It was not a shabby place, but a pleasantly furnished, elderly brownstone kept hospital-neat by its owners, two maiden sisters.

Mr. Jones lived in the room next to mine. My room was the smallest in the house, his the largest, a nice big sunshiny room, which was just as well, for Mr. Jones never left it: all his needs, meals, shopping, laundry, were attended to by the middle-aged landladies. Also, he was not without visitors; on the average, a half-dozen various persons, men and women, young, old, in-between, visited his room each day, from early morning until late in the evening. He was not a drug dealer or a fortune-teller; no, they came just to talk to him and apparently they made him small gifts of money for his conversation and advice. If not, he had no obvious means of support.

I never had a conversation with Mr. Jones myself, a circumstance I've often since regretted. He was a handsome man, about forty. Slender, black-haired, and with a distinctive face; a pale, lean face, high cheekbones, and with a birthmark on his left cheek, a small scarlet defect shaped like a star. He wore gold-rimmed glasses with pitch-black lenses: he was blind, and crippled, too – according to the sisters, the use of his legs had been denied him by a childhood accident, and he could not move without crutches. He was always dressed in a crisply pressed dark gray or blue three-piece suit and a subdued tie – as though about to set off for a Wall Street office.

However, as I've said, he never left the premises. Simply sat in his cheerful room in a comfortable chair and received visitors. I had no notion of why they came to see him, these rather ordinary-looking folk, or what they talked about, and I was far too concerned with my own affairs to much wonder over it. When I did, I imagined that his friends had found in him an intelligent, kindly man, a good listener in whom to confide and consult with over their troubles: a cross between a priest and a therapist.

Mr. Jones had a telephone. He was the only tenant with a private line. It rang constantly, often after midnight and as early as six in the morning.

I moved to Manhattan. Several months later I returned to the house to collect a box of books I had stored there. While the landladies offered me tea and cakes in their lace-covered 'parlor,' I enquired of Mr. Jones.

The women lowered their eyes. Clearing her throat, one said: 'It's in the hands of the police.'

The other offered: 'We've reported him as a missing person.'

The first added: 'Last month, twenty-six days ago, my sister carried up Mr. Jones's breakfast, as usual. He wasn't there. All his belongings were there. But he was gone.'

'It's odd –'

'– how a man totally blind, a helpless cripple –'

Ten years pass.

Now it is a zero-cold December afternoon, and I am in Moscow. I am riding in a subway car. There are only a few other passengers. One of them is a man sitting opposite me, a man wearing boots, a thick long coat and a Russian-style fur cap. He has bright eyes, blue as a peacock's.

After a doubtful instant, I simply stared, for even without the black glasses, there was no mistaking that lean distinctive face, those high cheekbones with the single scarlet star-shaped birthmark.

I was just about to cross the aisle and speak to him when the train pulled into a station, and Mr. Jones, on a pair of fine sturdy legs, stood up and strode out of the car. Swiftly, the train door closed behind him.

POCKET PENGUINS